**2ND EDITION**

BIG TV WORKBOOK

**Pearson Education Limited**
KAO Two
KAO Park
Harlow
Essex CM17 9NA
England
and Associated Companies throughout the world.

www.English.com/BigEnglish2

First published 2017

ISBN: 978-1-292-20363-8

Set in Heinemann Roman

Printed in Italy by L.E.G.O. S.p.A.

## Acknowledgements

The publisher would like to thank the following for their kind permission to reproduce their photographs:

(Key: b-bottom; c-centre; l-left; r-right; t-top)

**123RF.com:** 23Sudowoodo 23t (Marion), Aeaechan 15tr (girl looking at sign post), Akz 37tc, Julio Aldana 37tr, aleksvf 23c (airship), Alhovik 19c (planets), Allegresse 22tc, Ammit 14l, Andreypopov 29bc, Galyna Andrushko 20, Anolkil 36b, Atic12 28 (paranoia), Atosan 21cr, Leslie Banks 23bl, 31cr, Mariusz Blach 22tr, Maryna Bolsunova 19c (satellite), Karel Joseph Noppe Brooks 6, Alvaro Cabrera Jiménez 36t, Cristimatei 18c (satellite), Larry Cruikshank 34b, Comaniciu Dan 29bl, Aleksandr Davydov 25tc, Esteban De Armas 18t (Space colony), Sebastien Decoret 22bl, Denis Demidenko 35b, Dolgachov 26t (Earth sciences), Fazon 33 (Tower Bridge), funwayillustration 9tl, 9tr, Kadriya Gatina 23c (flying car), Get4net 11br, 27cr, Guesswho 28 (weather patterns), 31 (a), Darla Hallmark 31 (c), Highwaystarz 26b, Helen Hotson 13b, Maxim Ibragimov 4, Icetray 18c (ticket), Iimages 15b, Jehsomwang 27b, Iakov Kalinin 33 (Big Ben), Natthapong Khromkrathok 5r, Sergey Kohl 8c, Krmelda 28 (crop circle), Thanapol Kuptanisakorn 13l, 14cl, Yuliya Lapkovkaya 14r, Pavel Lunevich 19c (experiment), Stefano Marinari 33 (Leaning Tower of Pisa), Meinzahn 23br, 31cl, Roman Mikhailiuk 12, Teguh Mujiono 7t (Cathy), 7t (David), 7t (Ella), 7t (Frank), 7t (Gillian), Hendri Nguriana 15tr (boy relaxing), 15tr (shelter), Sergey Novikov 8b, 37b, Valeriy Novikov 39, Yana Ogonkova 23c (helicopter), Olaola 25b, Kostyantine Pankin 13cr, Natalia Pascari 23c (hot air balloon), Prykhodov 5l, Sergey Pykhonin 34t (Big Ben), 34t (Eiffel Tower), 34t (Great Wall of China), 34t (Statue of Liberty), 34t (Tower Bridge), 35tl (Big Ben), 35tl (Eiffel Tower), 35tl (Great Wall of China), 35tl (Statue of Liberty), 35tl (Tower Bridge), Somchai Rakin 10b, Rawpixel 22tl, Redkoala 38, Aubert Serge 25tl, 26t (pay gap), Mykhailo Shcherbyna 9b, Michael Sheehan 10cr, Sudowoodo 23t (Barton), 23t (Farrah), 23t (Mabel), 23t (Naresh), Suwoodo 27t (Anna), 27t (Benjy), 27t (Joseph), 27t (Suzanne), Tigatelu 11 (Laura), 11t (Buzz), 11t (Manny), 11t (Mary), tigatelu. 11t (Jack), Dinis Tolipov 29br, 30t (mathematician), Tsuneo 18c (Mars), Wamsler 31 (e), Wavebreak Media Ltd 26t (English), wavebreakmediamicro 5cr; **Pearson Education Ltd:** 7c (assignment), Danish Zaidi. Pearson India Education Services Pvt. Ltd 19t (Ben), 19t (Danna), 19t (Don), 19t (Matt), 19t (Shirley), Shivani Anshuk. Pearson India Education Services Pvt. Ltd 15tr (trek mountain), Jules Selmes 5b, 24; **Shutterstock.com:** Action Sports Photography 21r, Filatov Alexey 19c (Mars), AVAVA 8t, Bullwinkle 28 (man-made), 30t (man-made), Rich Carey 10cl, Jacek Chabraszewski 7bl, 19bl, Pavel Chagochkin 19c (futuristic city), Neale Cousland 32b, Colin D. Young 14b, Elen_Studio 31 (d), ER_09 28 (geometrical pattern), 30t (geometrical pattern), Gelpi JM 15cl, 35cl, Gpointstudio 37tl, Jorg Hackemann 33 (London Bridge), Chris Harvey 28 (UFO), 30b, Hogan Imaging 7br, 19br, Hung Chung Chih 33 (Great Wall of China), Sebastian Kaulitzki. 7c (computer), Deborah Kolb 15cr, 35cr, Sergii Korolko. 7c (website), Kuzma 10l, Kwest 10r, Marek CECH 17r, Rob Marmion 11bl, 27cl, Moneca 15tl (Bruce), 15tl (John), 15tl (Kathy), 15tl (Terri), Monkey Business Images 13r, 26t (science), Mylisa 17l, 18t (water), Ollyy 21b, Palych1378 22bc, Alexey Y. Petrov 21l, Narin Phapnam 18t (Oxygen tank), photocritical 32tl, PRILL 17c, Rawpixel.com 25tr, 26t (careers), Rtem 28 (radiation), 30t (radiation), Rvlsoft 7c (smartphone), Selecstock 32tr, SergeyDV 16, 18b, Victor Shova 21cl, Trinacria Photo 7c (research), Thor Jorgen Udvang 22br, Upthebanner 33 (Statue of Liberty), Kiselev Andrey Valerevich 5cl, Vasabii 27t (book), 27t (calculator), 27t (chemistry), 27t (globe), 27t (history), Wavebreakmedia 13cl, 14cr, WDG Photo 32tc, 33 (Eiffel Tower), Xzoex 23c (airplane), Albert Ziganshin 28 (aliens), 30t (aliens), 31 (b)

All other images © Pearson Education

# Contents

# Classroom Machines

I will learn about machines used in classrooms.

 **1** **Read and listen to the teacher talking to her class. What did she bring to show them?**

Good morning, class! Today, we're going to talk about how communication has changed over the years – and I've brought something special to show you. See this old phone? When I was a child, nobody had smartphones like we do today. Instead, we had these types of phones. To use them, you had to <u>lift the receiver</u>, then <u>press the number</u> on a keypad. It was very easy to <u>learn how to use</u> it – but you had to remember a lot of telephone numbers, which wasn't always that easy!

Right, so now let's talk about the assignments you have to do. You are going to <u>do some research</u> about how technology has changed over the last twenty years. For example, you can look at how the Internet was created and how people <u>develop websites</u> now, compared to twenty years ago. But don't worry, I will help you! If you <u>attend every class</u>, you'll do very well in this assignment.

**2** **Choose words from 1 and complete.**

**a** When you practice using a new machine you _____ it.

**b** When you get information about a topic you _____.

**c** When you make new Internet pages you _____.

**d** When you push a number on a keypad you _____.

**e** When you answer an old phone you have to _____.

**f** When you go to school you need to _____.

**3** **Listen and number in order. Then complete the sentences.**

online information ◯

individual research ◯

group project ◯

e-learning website ◯

**a** Have you found any _____ about languages classes yet? No, I'm looking on the Internet now.

**b** Sally, Gina, and I have started working on our _____, so we're going to the library to do some more research.

**c** Have you ever used an _____? Yes, I'm studying math online at the moment.

**d** We have to do _____ for this project. We're not supposed to do it in groups!

**4** **How does technology help you at school? Discuss and complete.**

**5** **What other technology do you use in your school? Make a list.**

BIG tv

**6** ▶ⓥⒾ **Watch. Number the phrases in the order you hear or see them.**

attend a class ☐    develop a website ☐    do research ☐

online information ☐    group projects ☐

**7** ▶ⓥⒾ **Watch again. Complete the table.**

| When | Technology |
|---|---|
| now (Singapore) | _____ |
| 1969 | _____ |
| 1934 | _____ |
| 1990s | _____ |
| now (Kenya) | _____ |

**8** **Read and complete. Then listen and check.**

projects    research    computers    e-learning    technological

In the 1990s, _____ might not have had the processing power they have today, but had already become useful tools in classrooms. They allowed students to do individual _____ and then develop group _____, using the teacher as a helper. Today, many schools use _____ support. Brian and Martin are in high school in Kenya. They grew up using computers and in their free time, they have developed an _____ website.

**9** **Ask and answer with a partner.**

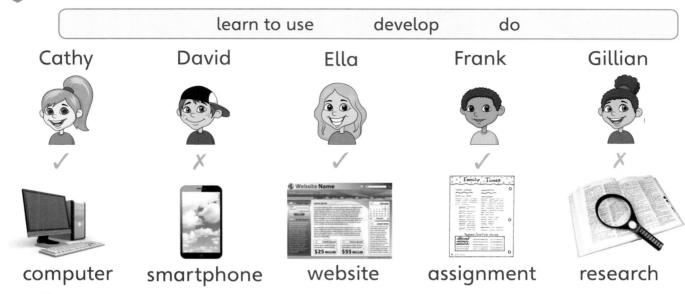

learn to use     develop     do

Cathy     David     Ella     Frank     Gillian

computer     smartphone     website     assignment     research

Has Cathy learned to use a computer yet?

Yes, she has. She has already learned to use a computer.

**5**
**10** **Write and match. Then listen and check.**

a  __Have__ you __done__ your assignment yet?

No, she _____. She _____ done it yet.

b  _____ Carol _____ hers?

I already _____!

c  _____ Bob and Ted _____ theirs?

Yes, they _____. They _____ already done it.

d  Let's go talk with Bob and Ted. Maybe they can help _____!

No, I __haven't__. I __haven't__ done it yet.

THINK BIG

Do you prefer print books or computers? Why? Talk with a partner.

# Saving the Environment

*I will learn about environmental issues.*

 **1** Read and listen about three school projects. Which one involves an alternative form of transport?

**1**

### Recycle Rangers

Join us in our clean-up project to help combat a serious <u>environmental problem</u>.

You too can be a Recycle Ranger and help to clean up our local parks and community spaces to improve the environment both for us and the local wildlife.

We'll pick up <u>garbage</u> and waste and take it to a recycling center, where we'll transform it into objects which can be useful to our community.

The Recycle Rangers meet at 4 p.m. every Wednesday outside the school library.

**2**

### Ocean Watch

Let's get together this fall and make a real difference to our beautiful coast!

We're a group of around 30 volunteers, and we meet every Saturday morning at 9 a.m. at the Center for Marine Life in Washington Square.

Come along and listen to presentations, watch videos, and get involved in projects to reduce <u>ocean pollution</u> and help save marine wildlife.

This Saturday we'll find out about an amazing invention which uses <u>ocean currents</u> to generate clean <u>energy</u>!

**3**

### Cycle to School Scheme

Are you interested in reducing <u>air pollution</u>?

Would you like to help save energy?

Are you keen to combat <u>climate change</u>?

Do you want to get fit, too?

It's easy – bring your bike to school!

To find out more about the benefits of the Cycle to School Scheme, pick up an information pack from the school admin office today.

**2** **Choose a word or phrase from 1. Write.**

**a** The gas, oil, and electricity we use. _____

**b** Things that have been thrown out. _____

**c** Waste that makes the atmosphere dirty and unsafe. _____

**d** Waste that makes the water dirty and unsafe. _____

**e** The movement of seawater. _____

**f** An issue or situation which has a negative effect on the planet. _____

**g** Long-term changes in the weather. _____

**3** **Listen, look, and say.**

cause

effect

**4** **What do you know about these environmental issues? Discuss and complete.**

| Environmental issue | Cause | Effects |
| --- | --- | --- |
| Deforestation | _____ | _____ |
| Global warming | _____ | _____ |
| Water pollution | _____ | _____ |
| Noise pollution | _____ | _____ |

**5** **What can you do to help the environment? Talk with a partner.**

**6** ▶ v2 **Watch. Check (✓) what you hear or see.**

garbage ☐

ocean pollution ☐

ocean currents ☐

climate change ☐

**7** ▶ v2 **Watch again. Complete the table.**

| Who | Issue | How are they getting involved? |
|---|---|---|
| Carrie | _____ | _____ |
| Boyan | _____ | _____ |
| School children | _____ | _____ |

**8** **Read and complete. Then listen and check.**

| plastic | currents | barrier | change | pollution | garbage |

Climate _____ is only one environmental problem we face. Ocean _____ is another. All over the world _____ dumped in the sea washes up on beaches. Boyan Slat has done more than worry. When he was nineteen years old, he had an idea. He suggested using the ocean _____ to get the oceans to clean themselves. His idea, a great floating _____ to catch the _____ as it is carried along by the currents, is being tested in the North Sea.

**9**  **Read and match. Ask and answer with a partner.**

**Help the planet with these good habits:**
- Ride a bike to school
- Recycle garbage
- Turn down the air conditioning
- Turn the lights off
- Use less paper
- Plant a tree
- Drive an electric car

 Mary wants to save energy.

 Jack loves gardening and wants to help the environment.

 Laura wants to reduce air pollution.

 Manny wants to save the forests.

 Buzz wants to reduce ocean pollution.

 What can Mary do to help the planet?

She can turn the lights off and turn down the air conditioning.

**10**  **Write and match.**

| What are | What kinds of | How can | What can |

a  <u>What are</u> current environmental problems?

We can use currents to get the oceans to clean themselves.

b  _____ we do to reduce the effects of climate change?

We can save energy.

c  _____ pollution are a problem?

Climate change is a big environmental problem.

d  _____ we clean the ocean?

Air pollution is one problem. Ocean pollution is another problem.

 **THINK BIG**

**What ideas do you have to reduce pollution? Brainstorm with your classmates.**

# 3 The Wild

## Before You Watch

I will learn about living in the wild

**1**  **Read and listen. Who is worried about the children not studying for the exams?**

**Dad:** Listen! What d'you think about this crazy idea? Alan's sports teacher wants to take the children to <u>live in the wild</u> for a week!

**Mom:** Oh, I'm all for it. Alan's fifteen now. It's important to get teenagers to <u>face a challenge</u>, isn't it? When I was that age, my parents wouldn't even let me <u>spend the night</u> in a tent in the yard!

**Dad:** But this is a week in a forest! They'll just <u>waste time</u> – no lessons, no homework – and exams start next month.

**Mom:** Oh come on! Just think what they'll learn. They're not allowed tents, so they'll have to make a plan and find out how to <u>build a shelter</u>.

**Dad:** Well, yes ok. But it's not just that. The teacher says he's going to make the children <u>climb a waterfall</u>!

**Mom:** What! Alan didn't tell me about that. That sounds dangerous! Perhaps we'd better go and discuss things with the school before we decide to let Alan go.

**2** **Choose a word or phrase from 1. Write.**

**a** Most giant pandas live in zoos, but some still _____.

**b** You will get very wet if you try to _____.

**c** Mike lives a long way from here. Ask his mom if you can _____ after the party.

**d** People who can't see _____ when doing ordinary jobs.

**e** I haven't got a tent, so I'll have to _____.

**f** Come on, we're late! Don't _____ playing games.

## 3 Listen, look, and say. Then complete the sentences.

make choices

work well together

cheat

encourage

**a** We're a great team and we _____.

**b** In the wild you have to _____ about what to do all the time.

**c** Our teachers always try to help us. They _____ us to do our best.

**d** You should never _____ in exams. It doesn't help you in the end.

## 4 What equipment would you need to live in the wild? Discuss and complete.

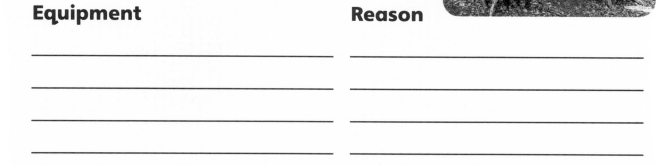

| Equipment | Reason |
|-----------|--------|
| _____ | _____ |
| _____ | _____ |
| _____ | _____ |
| _____ | _____ |

## 5 Would you like to live in the wild? Why or why not? Talk with a partner.

**6** ▶ⓥ³ **Watch. Check (✓) what you hear or see.**

climb a
waterfall ◯

make
choices ◯

work well
together ◯

build a
shelter ◯

**7** ▶ⓥ³ **Watch again. Then answer the questions.**

**a** How long will the teenagers be living in the wild? _____.

**b** What's wrong with the shelter the boys built? It's _____.

**c** What is Savannah scared of? She's scared of _____.

**d** Who gets up the waterfall? _____.

**e** At the end, what do the teenagers get as a reward?

_____ and _____.

 **8** **Read and complete. Then listen and check.**

| heights | plan | climb | choices | together |
|---|---|---|---|---|

It's morning – the girls find out they have won the task. They made good choices by listening to each other, making a _____, and working _____. The boys lost because they made some bad

_____. But today everyone in the team makes a brave decision. They will have to _____ this waterfall. This is not easy if you're scared of _____.

**9** **Ask and answer with a partner.**

 John

 Terri

 Kathy

 Bruce

| stay dry over night |
|---|

| have a great time in the wild |
|---|

| get to the top of the mountain more quickly |
|---|

| won't be able to make a fire while it gets dark |
|---|

 What will happen if John builds a shelter?

If John builds a shelter, he'll stay dry over night.

**10** **Write. Then listen and check.**

| If | don't listen | try your best | you explain | ~~pays attention~~ |
|---|---|---|---|---|
| if | you can do | I'll help | they won't | If ~~he'll know~~ |

**a** <u>If</u> Sam <u>pays attention</u>, <u>he'll know</u> what to do.

**b** _____ they _____ to their leader, _____ understand their tasks.

**c** _____ you _____, _____ almost anything.

**d** If _____ the problem to me, _____ you.

THINK BIG

**Do you think it is important to know how to make a fire? What other things are important to know how to do?**

Unit 3    **15**

# Mars Travel

## Before You Watch

**I will learn** about living on Mars.

**13**

**1** **Read and listen. Has the woman decided to go to Mars?**

**Dave:** We've looked at the photos of Mars, the red <u>planet</u>. They were actually taken from a <u>satellite</u> which is going around the planet. I have also told you about plans for a space <u>colony</u> of people from Earth in the future. So, the question is: Does anyone want to join this colony?

**Lexi:** Yes, I might be interested. I'm a journalist and I love adventure. I've traveled all over the world. The rocky <u>landscape</u> of Mars seems so strange and exciting! Do I need training to go to Mars?

**Dave:** Quite a lot, I'm afraid. You need to be strong, mentally and physically. You'd have to practice living alone in a spaceship <u>simulator</u> – that is a machine that copies how it feels to be in a spaceship. You'd have to live there for about a year! And you'd have to breathe <u>oxygen</u> from an oxygen tank.

**Lexi:** Well, I've already taken part in an <u>experiment</u> like that. I had to spend one week in a spaceship simulator. I have no problems using an oxygen tank to breathe. For example, I've climbed Mount Everest. I'm used to spending time on my own, too, because I've traveled by myself in wild and dangerous places.

**Dave:** I see. It sounds as if you might be the right person to go. But do you understand that you will never come back to Earth? The journey takes so long that it's a <u>one-way ticket</u> only.

**Lexi:** Oh ... I see. I didn't think of that. That makes a difference. I'll have to think about it again!

**2** **Choose a word or phrase from 1. Write.**

   **a** When you travel to a place and don't come back. _____

   **b** When a group of people settle in a new area. _____

   **c** The most important gas in the air for human life. _____

   **d** A machine used for training someone to live in certain conditions. _____

   **e** Earth and Mars. _____

   **f** What scientists do to test something. _____

   **g** A machine that travels around planets to get information. _____

   **h** An area of mountains, rivers, forests, or fields, for example. _____

**3** **Listen, look, and say.**

liquid water        organisms        survival

**4** **What do you know about space travel? Complete and discuss.**

| Event | Facts |
| --- | --- |
| first human on the moon | Apollo, Neil Armstrong, 1969 |
| _____ | _____ |
| _____ | _____ |
| _____ | _____ |

**5** **Would you like to go to Mars? Why or why not? Talk with a partner.**

**6** ▶ v4 **Watch. Number the pictures in the order you hear or see them.**

**7** ▶ v4 **Watch again. Match.**

| | | |
|---|---|---|
| **a** | liquid water | first colony on Mars |
| **b** | sending robots | organisms could survive |
| **c** | staying in simulator | since 1971 |
| **d** | Mars experiment | 520 days |
| **e** | Dutch company | 105 days in isolation |

**8** **Read and complete. Then listen and check.**

> landscape    water    organisms    satellite    1971

One of the most exciting recent discoveries was that liquid

_____ exists on Mars. It showed up in pictures taken

by a _____. Where there is water, there is life – or so

scientists believe. They think tiny _____ could survive

on Mars. If small organisms can survive on Mars,

maybe we can, too. Scientists have been sending

robots to investigate the planet's _____

and climate since _____.

**9** **Read and match. Then ask and answer with a partner.**

| Matt | | | a | live in a space colony |
| Danna | | | b | travel to other planets |
| Ben | | | c | do space experiments |
| Shirley | | | d | study the landscape of Mars |
| Don | | | e | work with satellites |

What will Matt be doing ten years from now?

He'll be living in a space colony.

**10** **Write. Then listen and check.**

**a Danny:** What <u>will</u> you <u>be</u> doing ten years from now?

**Sandy:** I _____ studying at a foreign university.

**b Danny:** Really? What _____ you _____ doing twenty years from now?

**Sandy:** I don't know. I _____ probably _____ living in a big city.

**c Sandy:** What _____ you _____ doing ten years from now?

**Danny:** I _____ definitely _____ working as a scientist.

**d Sandy:** And after that? What _____ you _____ doing twenty years from now?

**Danny:** I _____ living on another planet!

**THINK BIG**

What is your plan? What will you be doing ten years from now?

# 5 Up in the Air

## Before You Watch

I will learn about different flying machines.

**1** **Read and listen. Who has seen an airship?**

**Chris:** Wow! Just look at that <u>hot-air balloon</u>. Should we go for a ride?

**Amy:** I don't see what's so exciting about it. It's so much slower than an <u>airplane</u>.

**Chris:** Maybe, but hot-air balloons are such weird and wonderful <u>contraptions</u>. Think of the amazing view from up there! And they don't make much noise – not like <u>helicopters</u> or airplanes.

**Amy:** I guess you're right. My granddad once saw an <u>airship</u>, when he was a little boy. It was a bit like this hot-air balloon, but much longer and bigger, and it carried a lot more passengers. He said it was very exciting.

**Chris:** See? So how about that ride?

**Amy:** OK, why not? Let's have an adventure!

**Chris:** Great! When I was a little boy, I wanted to invent the first ever <u>flying car</u>. I even made a <u>prototype</u> out of boxes. Obviously, it didn't work ...

**Amy:** I also wanted to fly when I was a child, but not in a car. I wanted to be a <u>superhero</u>!

**2** **Choose a word or phrase from 1. Write.**

**a** A clever and unusual type of machine. _____

**b** A balloon, filled with hot air, that can carry people. _____

**c** A vehicle that flies and has one or more engines. _____

**d** An aircraft with large blades that turn very fast. _____

**e** An aircraft with a long balloon filled with gas. _____

**f** A character who uses special powers to help people. _____

**g** A car with wings that can travel in the air. _____

**h** A new type of machine that has just been invented. _____

## 3 Listen, look, and say. Then fill in the gaps, changing the word where necessary.

take off      motorized      transport      crash

This is the nine o'clock news. An airship to be used in a film about the early 20th century has _____ in a mountainous area. It _____ from Atlanta airport at ten a.m. and was _____ the film crew from Atlanta to Boston when it disappeared from the radar screen at about eleven o'clock. Air security explained that this airship – a hot-air balloon that has been _____ – is generally a very safe form of transport.

## 4 What superpowers would you like to have? Discuss and complete.

| Superpower | Reason |
|---|---|
| _____ | _____ |
| _____ | _____ |
| _____ | _____ |
| _____ | _____ |

## 5 What would you like to fly in? Why? Talk with a partner.

**6** ▶ (V5) **Watch. Number the pictures in the order you hear or see them.**

**7** ▶ (V5) **Watch again. Write the aircraft under the correct date.**

| airship | airplane | flying car | hot air balloon | helicopter |
|---|---|---|---|---|

| 1916 | 1920s | today | future |
|---|---|---|---|
| _____ | _____ | _____ | _____ |

_____

**8** **Read and complete. Then listen and check.**

| meters | fly | technology | superhero | jump |
|---|---|---|---|---|

Despite the advances of _____, we still haven't given up on flying like a _____. Every year, the International Birdman competition takes place in the UK. One man in the competition explains how it works: "What you are supposed to do is stand on the beach like this, and in a strong wind you _____ up and kick out." The participants jump off a pier and attempt to _____ using all kinds of contraptions. Tony Hughes won the competition by managing to fly for 85 _____ before crashing into the water.

**9** **Ask and answer with a partner.**

Mabel

Barton

Naresh

Farrah

Marion

If Mabel could travel by any vehicle, what would she choose?

If she could travel by any vehicle, she'd travel by hot-air balloon.

**10** **Match. Then listen and check.**

**a** If I could have one superpower, I'd see through walls.

If I didn't have to earn money, I'd write songs to make people happy.

**b** If you didn't have to go to work, what would you do every day?

If I could go anywhere, I'd go to the Great Barrier Reef in Australia.

**c** If you could go anywhere, where would you go?

See through walls? Why not fly or be very strong? If I were you, I'd choose something else.

**d** If you didn't have to earn money, what would you do all day?

If I didn't have to go to work, I would read books in the mornings and play basketball in the afternoons.

THINK BIG

**If you could have one superpower that nobody else had, what would it be? Why?**

# 6 Time for STEM

I will learn about science, technology, engineering, and math.

**1**  **Read and listen. What does Sally's brother say about girls? Does her teacher agree?**

**Teacher:** Hi, Sally. I've asked all the final-year students to come and see me so we can talk about their careers. Maybe I can help you with some advice. What do you think you'd like to study at college?

**Sally:** That's very kind of you, Mr. Thompson. Actually, I need some advice. I'm no good at <u>history</u> and English. What I'm really good at is <u>science</u>. And I got high marks in <u>geography</u> too, and in <u>math</u>. But my brother says most science students at college are boys, and that girls aren't very good at science and can't find jobs. Anyway, I'm good at math but don't really enjoy it, so I suppose science is out.

**Teacher:** Your brother's just teasing you, Sally. There are lots of great women scientists. And these days, more and more girls are studying <u>engineering</u> and <u>technology</u> too! Have you ever thought of studying Earth sciences?

**Sally:** I don't really know what that is.

**Teacher:** It's subjects like geography, <u>geology</u>, and ecology – subjects that study the environment. You don't need advanced math, and there are quite a lot of job opportunities.

**Sally:** That sounds great! Where can I find out more about it?

**Teacher:** Go online and look up different colleges and see what's on their program. Oh, and there's a video I could send you if you like.

**2** **Choose a word or phrase from 1. Write.**

**a** The study of numbers, quantities, and shapes. _____

**b** The study of the past. _____

**c** The study of how things like roads or bridges are built. _____

**d** The study of scientific or industrial methods to make new things. _____

**e** The study of countries, cities, mountains, etc. _____

**f** The study of the natural world based on facts and experiments. _____

**g** The study of the Earth and its rocks. _____

**3** **Listen, look, and say. Then complete the sentences.**

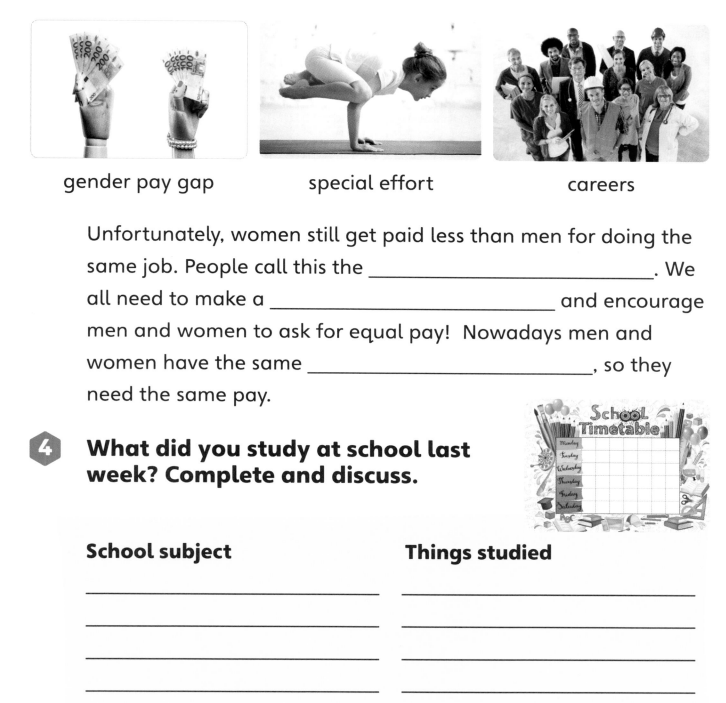

gender pay gap                    special effort                    careers

Unfortunately, women still get paid less than men for doing the same job. People call this the _____. We all need to make a _____ and encourage men and women to ask for equal pay! Nowadays men and women have the same _____, so they need the same pay.

**4** **What did you study at school last week? Complete and discuss.**

| School subject | Things studied |
|---|---|
| _____ | _____ |
| _____ | _____ |
| _____ | _____ |
| _____ | _____ |

**5** **What do you think is the most important subject at school? Why? Talk with a partner.**

**6**  **Watch. Check (✓) what you hear or see.**

 science ☐  English ☐  gender pay gap ☐  Earth sciences ☐  careers ☐

**7**  **Watch again. Match.**

| | | |
|---|---|---|
| **a** | Brian Cox | invited 500 school girls |
| **b** | Michelle Obama | UK young scientist award |
| **c** | Royal Institution | science can be astonishing |
| **d** | Techcamp in Togo | inspiring women and girls |
| **e** | Roxanne | how to build a computer |

**8**  **Read and complete. Then listen and check.**

| science | STEM | engineering | lessons | designs |
|---|---|---|---|---|

University technical colleges in the UK also give girls a chance to see a more practical side of _____. One student at this kind of college said, "I like _____ because it's a way that I can express myself and you actually get to see your _____ built up." School life at these colleges combines practical and normal _____ including English, history, and geography as well as the _____ subjects.

**10** **Ask and answer with a partner. Use the words in the box.**

| more | the most | fewer | the fewest |

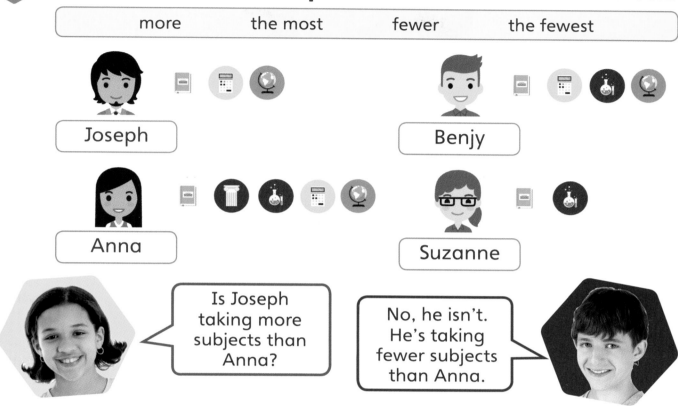

Joseph

Benjy

Anna

Suzanne

Is Joseph taking more subjects than Anna?

No, he isn't. He's taking fewer subjects than Anna.

 **11** **Choose. Then listen and check.** 24

a Practical experiments **make / don't make** science fun.

b In most countries, **men / women** earn more than **men / women**.

c If **girls / boys** are interested in STEM subjects, they may get **better / worse** paid jobs later.

d "We need strong, smart, **confident / pretty** young women," Michelle Obama said.

 **What do you want to do for your career? How do you need to prepare?**

# 7 Mystery: Crop Circles

## Before You Watch

I will learn about the mystery of crop circles.

 25

**1** **Listen, number, and say.**

weather patterns ◯

aliens ◯

man-made ◯

paranoia ◯

crop circle ◯

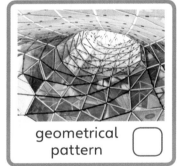

geometrical pattern ◯

UFO ◯

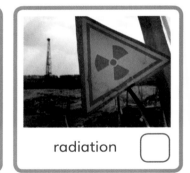

radiation ◯

**2** **Choose a word or phrase from 1. Write.**

**a** Creatures from space. _____

**b** A flying object from space. _____

**c** A large pattern found in a field. _____

**d** A pattern made from lines and shapes. _____

**e** A feeling that people are trying to hurt you. _____

**f** A combination of weather systems. _____

**g** A thing made by people. _____

**h** A dangerous energy coming from chemicals. _____

## 3 Read and complete. Then listen and check.

**Judy:** Hey, Tom, I saw this fantastic thing in the sky last night – like a very bright star, but it was changing color all the time. Do you think it was a _____?

**Tom:** Oh come on! You don't believe in flying machines from other planets, do you? Or _____ looking like little green men?

**Judy:** Well, I suppose not. But what else could it be?

**Tom:** Probably something scientists have invented. A _____ object, in other words!

**Judy:** I suppose you're right. But it could really be dangerous then, and produce _____ or something poisonous!

**Tom:** That's just _____! You think everything is dangerous and it's going to hurt you. That's just not true!

**Judy:** OK, then. Perhaps I was just dreaming. But what about this other thing that I heard about on the radio? A weird _____ appeared during the night in a field near here. They call it a _____ because it's round, like a circle, and it's in a farmer's field.

**Tom:** Oh, that? I think it's just because of changing _____. You know, when we first had those strong winds, then no wind at all. You shouldn't believe everything you hear!

## 4 Do you agree with Tom? What do you think makes crop circles? Why? Talk with a partner.

## 5 Listen, look, and say.

geochemist          psychologist

mathematician

## 6 Which of the three people in 4 do you think has the most interesting job? Complete the sentence.

I think _____ has the most interesting job, because

_____.

**7** ▶(V7) **Watch. Check (✓) what you hear or see.**

 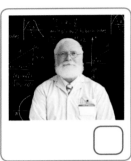   

**8** ▶(V7) **Watch again. Match.**

| | |
|---|---|
| **a** group of artists | 151 circles |
| **b** famous crop circle | tests the soil in crop circles |
| **c** Geochemist Mark Hodson | reproduce circles |
| **d** scientist Christopher French | believes human psychology explains crop circles |

**9** (28) **Read and complete with words from the box. Then listen and check.**

| mysterious | set | causes | circles | crops | believe |
|---|---|---|---|---|---|

Another mystery: crop circles. They appear every year. People wonder what _____ these geometrical patterns of flattened cereal _____. Most appear in the dead of night, and are believed to have _____ origins and even mystical powers. Are they made by humans, unknown weather patterns, or even aliens? Crop circle researchers _____ that most circles are too sophisticated to be man-made. This is the layout of the Julia _____, a famous crop circle that appeared in the UK, made up of 151 _____.

**10** **Match. Ask and answer with a partner.**

a

b

c

d

e

| can be dangerous | isn't it? |
| is man-made | can't it? |
| haven't been seen here | aren't they? |
| couldn't have made the crop circles | could they? |
| are changing | have they? |

Weather patterns are changing, aren't they?

Yes, I believe they are!

**29**
**11** **Write and match. Then listen and check.**

a Stonehenge is in England, <u>isn't it</u>?

b Crop circles usually appear in cereal crops, _____?

c You haven't seen an alien, _____?

d He's not paranoid, _____?

Yes, they do.

No, I haven't!

Yes, it is.

Yes, he is!

**THINK BIG**

Do you believe in aliens? Why or why not? Talk with a partner.

# Moving Landmarks

I will learn about different landmarks.

 **1 Listen, look, and say.**

structure

original

replica

**2** **What do you know about these landmarks? Discuss and complete.**

| Landmark | Where is it? |
| --- | --- |
| Eiffel Tower | _____ |
| Taj Mahal | _____ |
| Machu Picchu | _____ |
| Big Ben | _____ |
| Leaning Tower of Pisa | _____ |

**3** **What landmark would you most like to see? Why? Talk with a partner.**

## 4 Listen, number, and fill in the missing word.

Great _____ of China ◯

Eiffel _____ ◯

_____ of Liberty ◯

_____ Bridge ◯

Leaning _____ of Pisa ◯

Tower _____ ◯

Big _____ ◯

## 5 Choose a word or phrase from 1. Write.

a One of the world's most famous landmarks is the _____. This is a metal tower right in the centre of Paris.

b There are a lot of famous landmarks in London. _____ is a bell, next to the Houses of Parliament, that rings every hour. And _____ is a famous bridge across the River Thames. It has two tall towers.

c _____ is another famous bridge. But the original one is not in London – it's actually in Arizona, USA!

d When people came to New York on a ship, the first thing they saw was a huge statue called the _____.

e When buildings aren't straight, they will fall, won't they? Not necessarily. The _____ in Italy has been leaning over for hundreds of years – without crashing to the ground!

f The _____ is an amazing sight. It was built thousands of years ago to protect the Chinese states.

**6** ▶ v8  **Watch. Number the pictures in the order you hear or see them.**

  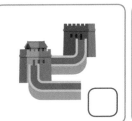  

**7** ▶ v8  **Watch again. Complete the table.**

| Landmark | Details |
|---|---|
| _____ | symbol of freedom |
| _____ | also designed by Gustave Eiffel |
| _____ | often confused with London Bridge |
| _____ | a lifesize replica |
| _____ | starting to lean |

**32**

**8**  **Read and complete with words from the box. Then listen and check.**

| Atlantic | Bridge | Arizona | Thames | Tower Bridge |
|---|---|---|---|---|

Back in 1968, London _____ was getting ready for a long journey. It was sold, taken apart in pieces, and then transported across the _____, all the way to _____, in the USA, where it was rebuilt. Legend says the American buyer made a mistake and thought he had purchased the more impressive _____, often confused with London Bridge. He denied it. In any case, the London Bridge over the River _____ today is not the original.

**9** **Match. Ask and answer with a partner.**

Big Ben

Great Wall of China

Eiffel Tower

Statue of Liberty

Tower Bridge

built more than two thousand years ago

designed by Alexandre Gustave Eiffel

renamed the Elizabeth Tower in 2012

across the River Thames

in New York

What do you know about Big Ben?

The tower of Big Ben was renamed the Elizabeth Tower in 2012.

**10** **Write. Then listen and check.**

| destroy | build | paint | form | ~~complete~~ |

**a** The Eiffel Tower <u>**was completed**</u> in 1889.

**b** The pyramids in Mexico _____ by the Mayans three thousand years ago.

**c** The Colossus of Rhodes _____ by an earthquake in 226 BC.

**d** The Mona Lisa _____ in about 1504 CE.

**e** The Himalayan mountains _____ many millions of years ago.

**THINK BIG**

**What is your favorite landmark in your own country? When was it built?**

# q Amazing Gaming

## Before You Watch

I will learn about the past and future of gaming.

### 1 Read and listen.

One of the first successful <u>video games</u> was Space Invaders. People had to go to an <u>arcade</u> to play it. In those days you didn't play games at home. Now people play games like <u>Pokémon GO</u>™ on their own <u>devices</u> – usually their smartphones. Games today also have a lot of interesting <u>characters</u> that the players can relate to.

Gaming has become very popular. A lot of games involve <u>virtual reality</u>, so you actually think you are in a real environment and not just an imaginary one. There are fan <u>conventions</u> where hundreds of gamers go to discuss their games. And becoming a <u>game developer</u> is now a very popular career choice, because you have to create new games all the time!

### 2 Choose a word or phrase from 1. Write.

a Someone who makes a game. _____

b A place where people go to play electronic games.

_____

c A large meeting. _____

d Clever machines you can use for things like playing games.

_____

e People who appear in a game, film, or story. _____

f A simulated world created by a computer. _____

g An app-based game involving moving around. _____

h An old type of electronic game. _____

### 3 Listen, look, and say.

fan culture

addictive

event

### 4 Write.

There's a real _____ culture around gaming. People who love it, go to _____ to play and talk about their favorite games – and meet other enthusiasts. But some people say gaming is bad for you because it can be very _____.

### 5 What games have you played? Describe them. Discuss and complete.

| Game | Description |
|------|-------------|
| _____ | _____ |
| _____ | _____ |
| _____ | _____ |
| _____ | _____ |

### 6 What is the best game you've ever played? Why? Tell a partner. Explain how to play it.

**7** ▶(vq) **Watch. Check (✓) what you hear or see.**

Space Invaders ☐    game developers ☐    arcade ☐

virtual reality ☐    devices ☐

characters ☐    fan culture ☐

**8** ▶(vq) **Watch again. Complete the table.**

| Who | How they described gaming |
|---|---|
| Two boys in Hong Kong | _____ |
| Girl in green top | _____ |
| Girl dressed as Lulu | _____ |
| Girl with glasses | _____ |

**9** (36)(🎧) **Read and complete. Then listen and check.**

| virtual | hug | Developers | Space | games |

_____ have created _____ that appeal to our sense of touch. Users wear a special vest. When they _____ the mannequin, it actually feels like the mannequin is hugging back. Gaming has come a long way since _____ Invaders. In the future, _____ reality will enable us to "live" a vast range of experiences or even completely different lives within a game environment.

**10** **Read. Then write. Listen and check.**

**a** STELLA — "I love Pokémon Go™!"

**b** PETER — "I want to dress as my favorite character."

**c** JACINTA — "I've never heard of Space Invaders."

**d** BOBBY — "I'm meeting Sam at the arcade."

**e** JANET — "I want to be a game developer in the future."

**a** Stella said she <u>loved Pokémon GO™</u> .

**b** Peter said he _____.

**c** Jacinta said she _____.

**d** Bobby said he _____.

**e** Janet said she _____.

 **11** **Write and match. Then listen and check.**

**a** Cynthia said, "I am meeting Sarah at the arcade." — Cynthia said she <u>was meeting</u> Sarah at the arcade.

**b** Tommy said, "We are dressing up as characters to go to the convention!"

Damien said they _____ _____ to the movies.

**c** Rachel said, "I'm reading a new book on my device."

Tommy said they _____ _____ up as characters to go to the convention.

**d** Damien said, "We're going to the movies."

Rachel said she _____ _____ a new book on her device.

**THINK BIG** What has someone told you recently? Tell a partner. Begin: X told me that he/she …

# Word List

## 1 Classroom Machines

attend every class
develop a website
do research
learn how to use
lift the receiver
press the number
e-learning website
group project
individual research
online information

## 2 Saving the Environment

air pollution
climate change
energy
environmental problem
garbage
ocean currents
ocean pollution
cause
effect

## 3 The Wild

build a shelter
climb a waterfall
face a challenge
live in the wild
spend the night
waste time
cheat
encourage
make choices
work well together

## 4 Mars Travel

colony
experiment
landscape
one-way ticket
oxygen
planet
satellite
simulator
liquid water
organisms
survival

## 5 Up in the Air

airplane
airship
contraption
flying car
helicopter
hot-air balloon
prototype
superhero
crash (v)
motorized
take off (v)
transport (v)

## 6 Time for STEM

engineering
geography
geology
history
math
science
technology
career
gender pay gap
special effort

## 7 Mystery: Crop Circles

aliens
crop circle
geometrical pattern
man-made
paranoia
radiation
UFO
weather patterns
geochemist
mathematician
psychologist

## 8 Moving Landmarks

Big Ben
Eiffel Tower
Great Wall of China
Leaning Tower of Pisa
London Bridge
Statue of Liberty
Tower Bridge
original
replica
structure

## 9 Amazing Gaming

arcade
characters
convention
devices
game developer
Pokémon GO™
video game
virtual reality
addictive
event
fan culture